Saddle Up!

By Mary Iverson

Welcome to the Studio!

To jump right into the saddle, turn to page 4.

Saddle Up!

©2008 becker&mayer! LLC

Published by SmartLab®, an imprint of becker&mayer!
All rights reserved. SmartLab® and ArtLab® are registered trademarks of becker&mayer!,
11120 NE 33rd Place, Suite 101, Bellevue, Washington.
Creative development by Jim Becker, Anna Johnson, and Aaron Tibbs

No part of this book may be reproduced, stored in a retrieval system, or transmitted in any form or by any means, electronic, mechanical, photocopying, recording, or otherwise, without the prior permission of SmartLab®. Requests for such permissions should be addressed to SmartLab® Permissions, becker&mayer!, 11120 NE 33rd Place, Suite 101, Bellevue, WA 98004.

If you have any questions or comments about this product, please visit www.smartlabtoys.com/customerservice.html and click on the Customer Service Request Form.

Edited by Nancy Waddell
Written and illustrated by Mary Iverson
Art direction and packaging design by Eddee Helms
Design assistance by Tyler Freidenrich
Production art by Nathan Cavanaugh and Tyler Freidenrich
ArtLab® character and product photography by Keith Megay
Product photography by Jeff Miller
Product development by Breanna Guidotti
Project and production management by Beth Lenz
Photo research by Zena Chew
Special thanks to Kiah Helms and Sara DeBell

Printed, manufactured, and assembled in China, May 2009
at Winner Printing & Packaging Ltd.

Saddle Up! is part of the
ArtLab® Horse Drawing Studio kit.
Not to be sold separately.

2 3 4 5 6 13 12 11 10 09
ISBN-13 978-1-60380-004-4
ISBN-10 1-60380-004-2
09225

Photo Credits: Page 2: *Bay by the Bay* © Nakisha E. VanderHoeven. Page 3: Leonardo da Vinci horse sketch, image © Dover Publications, Inc.; horse graffiti, image © Mònica Tudela. Page 6: *The Horse in Motion*, Eadweard Muybridge, The Library of Congress. Page 7: Oldenburg horse © Bob Langrish / Dorling Kindersley / Getty Images. Page 12: cave painting, Grotte Lascaux, image © bunzyke007, Flickr. Page 16: *Appaloosa* © Renata Alvadia. Page 20: *Le Cirque*, Georges Seurat, image © Erich Lessing / Art Resource, NY; Lipizzaner horse © Christopher Pillitz / Reportage / Getty Images. Page 24: *The Unicorn in Captivity*, image © The Metropolitan Museum of Art / Art Resource, NY; Arabian horse © Tim Flanch / Stone / Getty Images. Page 28: *Ryuko No Uma*, The Library of Congress. Page 30: *Little Blue Horse*, Franz Marc, image © The Bridgeman Art Library / Getty Images; bucking foal © Dusty Perin.

Harness Your Talent

Horses are beautiful animals whose grace and power have been the subject of artwork by such great artists as Leonardo da Vinci (drawing at right) and Pablo Picasso. But you can also see them used today, like in the graffiti art photographed below.

Horses can be difficult to capture in a drawing. The instructions in this book break down the process into simple steps. And you'll learn how to use horse models, just like an artist.

You'll draw all kinds of horses in different poses. After you've mastered the basics, you'll learn how to draw unicorns, make abstract art, and even create cartoons.

Stable of Contents

Coat of Many Colors	4
Out of the Gait!	6
Beauti-foal	12
Giddyup!	16
Arena Patina	20
Fantastical	24
Cartoon Corral	28
Letting Go of the Reins	30
Round-up	32

Well Read

Horses also inspired writers. *Black Beauty* and *Misty of Chincoteague* are classic tales about our equine friends.

COAT OF MANY COLORS

Your kit has all the tools you need to learn how to draw horses, including two horse models and a stand. You also get pastels and colored pencils. With these, you can add color and texture to your horse drawings.

Models
Artists use models like these to help visualize a person or animal. The two horse models—an adult and a foal—will help you see where all of the parts of the horse should be.

Graphite Pencil
Use this pencil to sketch out your horses and to add details to your final drawings.

Stand
The stand will keep your model in its pose and allow you to easily see the horse from all angles. It fits both models.

Smudger
Use the smudger to soften or blur your pencil and pastel marks.

Eraser
Use the eraser to remove unwanted pencil lines or create texture with pastels.

REALITY CHECK
Reality checks appear throughout the book. They show how a drawing looks on top of the model pose. Check your work against these photos as you draw.

Pastels

Pastels are soft, blendable sticks of colored pigment. When you rub a pastel stick on your paper, it crumbles a little bit. This leaves behind bits of powdery color. There are many ways to use a pastel stick to get smooth or textured results.

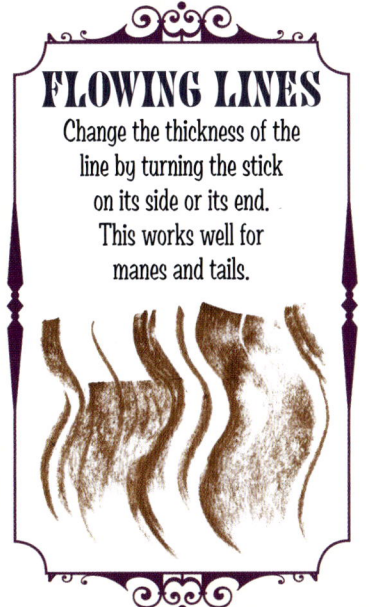

Ochre
Brown
Red
Purple
Blue
Green

FLOWING LINES
Change the thickness of the line by turning the stick on its side or its end. This works well for manes and tails.

SMOOTH COATS
Create horse coats and backgrounds with pastels.

Blend red and ochre pastel for a chestnut coat.

Blend ochre pastel for the dusty ground.

Add marks on top for dirt and rocks.

CROSSHATCHING
To build up background colors, use crosshatching.

Add other colors to give it the texture of grass.

Colored Pencils

Colored pencils are good for making lines and textured marks that you don't want blended together. They give you more control than pastels because the pigment is held together with glue-like materials, and then soaked in wax. This keeps the pigment from blending on your paper.

TEXTURE
To create texture, place your paper over a rough surface.

For an Appaloosa coat, try a piece of sandpaper.

Try these other rough surfaces for a variety of textured effects.

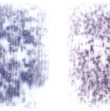

Wood Table   Can Lid   Wall

SHARP LINES

You can use colored pencils to create the sharp outline of a hoof.

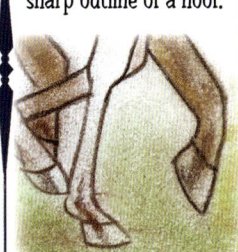

Colored pencils can add texture over a blended pastel coat.

Use colored pencils to darken shadow areas, like the grass under this fence.

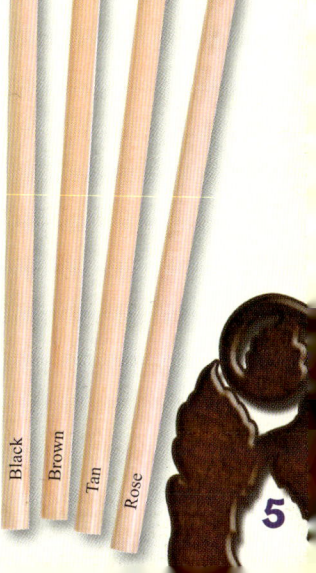

Black
Brown
Tan
Rose

5

OUT OF THE GAIT!

Horses move at four different natural gaits. They can walk, trot, canter, or gallop. Galloping is the fastest. Each gait has a pattern to how many hooves hit the ground from moment to moment. Look at these photos of horses at each of the different gaits. Play with putting your model into all of the poses.

The Horse in Motion, Eadweard Muybridge, 1878.
Muybridge captured this horse in motion to prove that when a horse canters or gallops, there is a moment when all four hooves can be off the ground at the same time.

WALK
This American Quarter Horse lifts up one hoof at a time as it walks. A walking horse will always have three of its feet on the ground.

TROT
At a trot, this Akhal-Teke springs forward off two hooves at a time. The hooves lifted are diagonal from each other.

CANTER
At a canter, this Appaloosa touches down one back hoof, then a diagonal pair of hooves, then the remaining front hoof before it is in the air again.

GALLOP
A gallop is like a canter, only faster! At a gallop, this Brabant is in the air most of the time. It pushes itself forward by touching one foot down at a time.

Grand-stand

The first project is a horse in a standing pose. Using the photo to the right as your guide, pose your model. The lines of the neck and back are fluid and graceful. All four legs are visible.

French Saddle Horse

The French Saddle Horse (Selle Français) breed is strong, but elegant. These horses are great athletes that excel in show jumping competition.

Pose

🐾 First, put the adult horse model on the stand.

🐾 Move the head so it is up and looking forward.

🐾 Move the legs so they are straight.

Anatomy

Some horse body parts have special names you may not know. We use these terms throughout the book, so get familiar with them by studying this image.

Labels: Mane, Flank, Withers, Ear, Eye, Nostril, Muzzle, Shoulder, Tail, Hocks, Knees, Pastern, Fetlock, Hoof

HIS-TOE-RY

Prehistoric horses didn't have hooves. Instead, they had three toes on each foot.

Body

The main body is built by using circles.

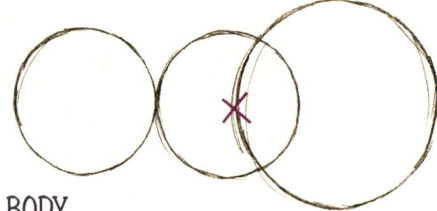

REALITY CHECK

BODY
- Starting in the center of your paper, draw two circles side-by-side. One is for the horse's middle, and one is for its back.
- Draw a larger circle in front that overlaps the middle circle right at its center.

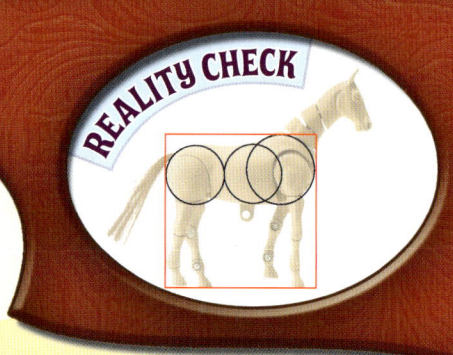

ESTIMATE YOUR PROPORTIONS
You've just drawn circles for the body. Now use a square to estimate where the legs will be.

HOW TO DRAW A SQUARE:
- Draw a line across the top of your circles.
- Lay your pencil on top of this line with the tip at one end and your thumb at the other.
- Use this measurement to find the length of the other sides of your square.
- Mark the corners of the square, then draw in the lines.

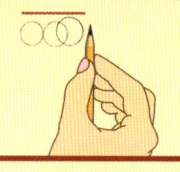

Head & Upper Legs

Use small circles to locate the head and the leg joints.

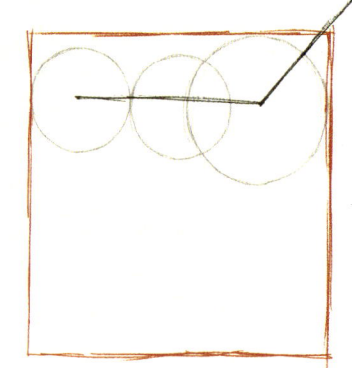

ART TIP!
In each step throughout the book, look at the darkest lines of the illustration. These lines refer to that step's directions.

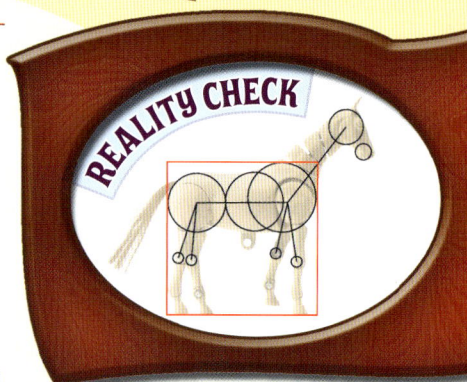

REALITY CHECK

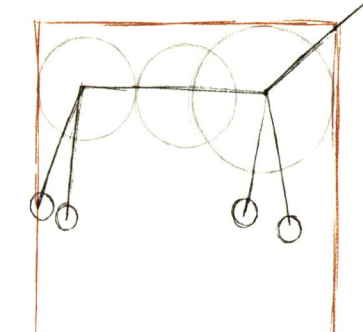

EQUAL DISTANCE
- Draw a line from the center of the back circle to the center of the front circle.
- Draw a line of equal length from the center of the front circle toward where the head will be.

HEAD
- Draw a circle for the head, and one for the tip of the nose, or muzzle.

UPPER LEGS
- Draw lines for the upper legs. The lines point down from the center of the front and back circles.
- Add small circles to the ends of your upper leg lines. These are the knees and hocks.

Lower Legs & Contours

Now it's time to connect all your lines to form the basic outline of a horse.

ART TIP!
Erase away! If at any point you are not happy with how your drawing looks, use your eraser!

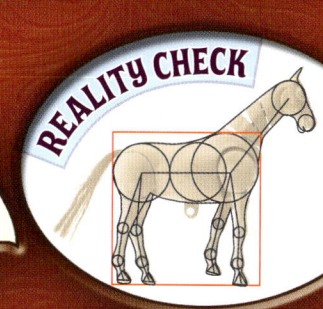

REALITY CHECK

LOWER LEGS
- Draw lines pointing down from the knee circles. Look at your model for the angles.
- Add circles for the ankle joints, called fetlocks.
- Draw four short lines that angles forward from the fetlocks. These are the pasterns.
- Draw triangles for the hooves.

CONTOURS
- Sketch the contours of the horse's head, body, and legs.

Outline

After you've sketched your horse, you'll create a clean line drawing of it. First, by outlining it with colored pencil and then by erasing the sketchy graphite pencils lines.

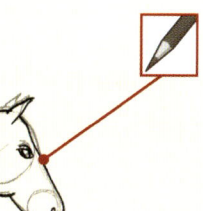

SHAPE
- With a black colored pencil, draw one thick outline over your best sketchy lines.

ART TIP!
Colored pencil lines don't erase as easily as the graphite pencil lines. This is why you use the graphite pencil to sketch and the colored pencil for the outline of your horse.

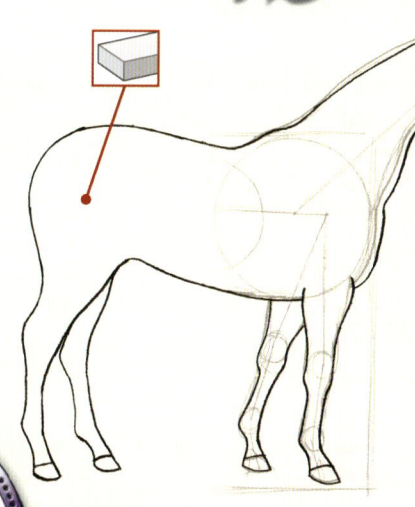

ERASE
- Erase all your sketchy pencil lines for a clean line drawing of your standing horse.

9

Details

🐾 Draw all the features of the horse. Here they are up close. For more ideas, refer back to the horse photo on page 7.

Tail, Mane, Ears, Eye, Nostril, Hoof

EYE SEE
Horses have better night vision than humans.

Color

Our inspirational photo is of a Dark Bay French Saddle Horse (Selle Francais). It is reddish-brown with a dark brown mane and tail.

BASE COLOR
🐾 Use brown pastel to fill in the horse's body. Create a light, blended coat of brown using the side of the pastel.

🐾 Leave some white paper showing through. This will give your drawing more depth.

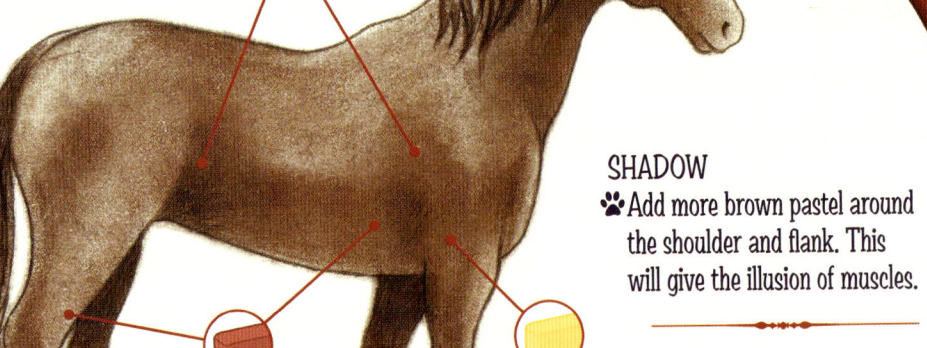

SHADOW
🐾 Add more brown pastel around the shoulder and flank. This will give the illusion of muscles.

SHADING
🐾 Use red pastel over these darkened areas. Blend from dark to light.

🐾 Add some ochre pastel in the lighter areas.

10

Final Stage

Your standing horse is just about done. Now it's time to add the final details and a fun background.

DARKEN
Add more brown pastel and brown colored pencil to darken the legs and shadow areas.

SMOOTH IT OUT
Blend black pastel into the mane, tail, legs, and shadow areas.

DEFINE
Add black and brown colored pencil to define the eyes, nose, and mouth.

SHADOW
Use brown pastel to create a shadow under your horse.

BACKGROUND
Now that your horse is complete, create a pastoral background. Here we used green, blue, and brown pastel, as well as the graphite pencil.

GO WILD

Side Saddle
Try coloring your standing horse like an Appaloosa. Add a saddle.

Yarn Spin
Add yarn to the mane and tail for a 3-D effect.

Beauti-Foal

A foal is a baby horse. A pony is a type of small-sized horse, such as a Shetland, of any age. Foals are smaller than adult horses, of course. But, they also have different proportions. The biggest difference between an adult and baby horse is the legs. A foal's legs are spindly compared to the rest of its body.

Paleolithic fresco, Great Hall of the Bulls, Grotte Lascaux, France.

Artists used crushed burnt sticks, crumbled red rocks, and spit to create this fresco—and it's lasted more that 17,000 years! It is thought that prehistoric hunters painted these types of pictures for good luck in helping them bring home a lot of food for the camp fire.

Pose

Since a foal's body is smaller than that of an adult horse's body, your circles will be different than in the Out of the Gait! project.

- Put the foal model on the stand.
- Move the legs into a walking position.

Quarter Horses

Quarter Horses are able to turn sharply and quickly. They are popular in all equine sports that require a short burst of speed. In fact, the Quarter Horse was named because of how fast it can run a quarter mile (.4km).

PERFECT CIRCLE

You can trace a quarter to make the two smaller circles for the foal's body. A fifty-cent piece is the perfect size for the larger circle.

STAND UP!

Newborn foals can stand within an hour of birth!

Body & Head

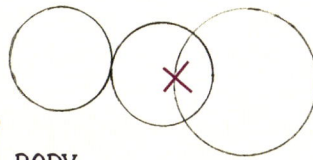

BODY
- Draw two circles side-by-side, one for the foal's middle and one for its back.
- Draw a larger circle in front that overlaps the middle circle at its center.

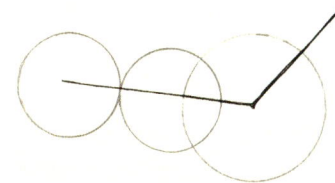

EQUAL DISTANCE
- Draw a line from the center of the back circle to the center of the front circle.
- Draw a line of equal length toward where the head will be.

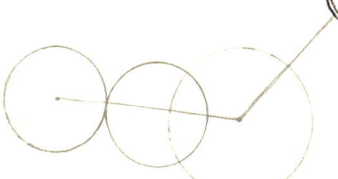

HEAD
- Draw a circle at the top of the neck line. This is the head.
- Draw a smaller circle for the muzzle.

REALITY CHECK

Legs

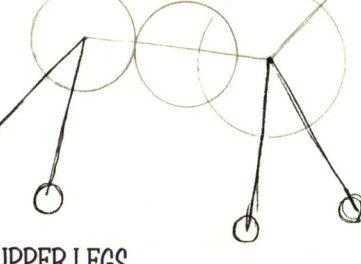

UPPER LEGS
- Draw two lines that start at the center of the back circle.
- Draw two lines that start at the center of the front circle.
- Draw small circles at the ends of your first leg lines for the knees and hocks.

LOWER LEGS
- Draw a line pointing downward from each knee and each hock. These are the lower legs.
- Draw small circles at the end of each lower leg. These are the fetlocks.
- Draw four short lines for the pasterns and triangles for the hooves.

REALITY CHECK

KNEE BENDS
In front, the joints are called "knees." In back, these joints are called "hocks." The front legs bend at the knees like a human's legs. The hind legs bend in the opposite direction.

13

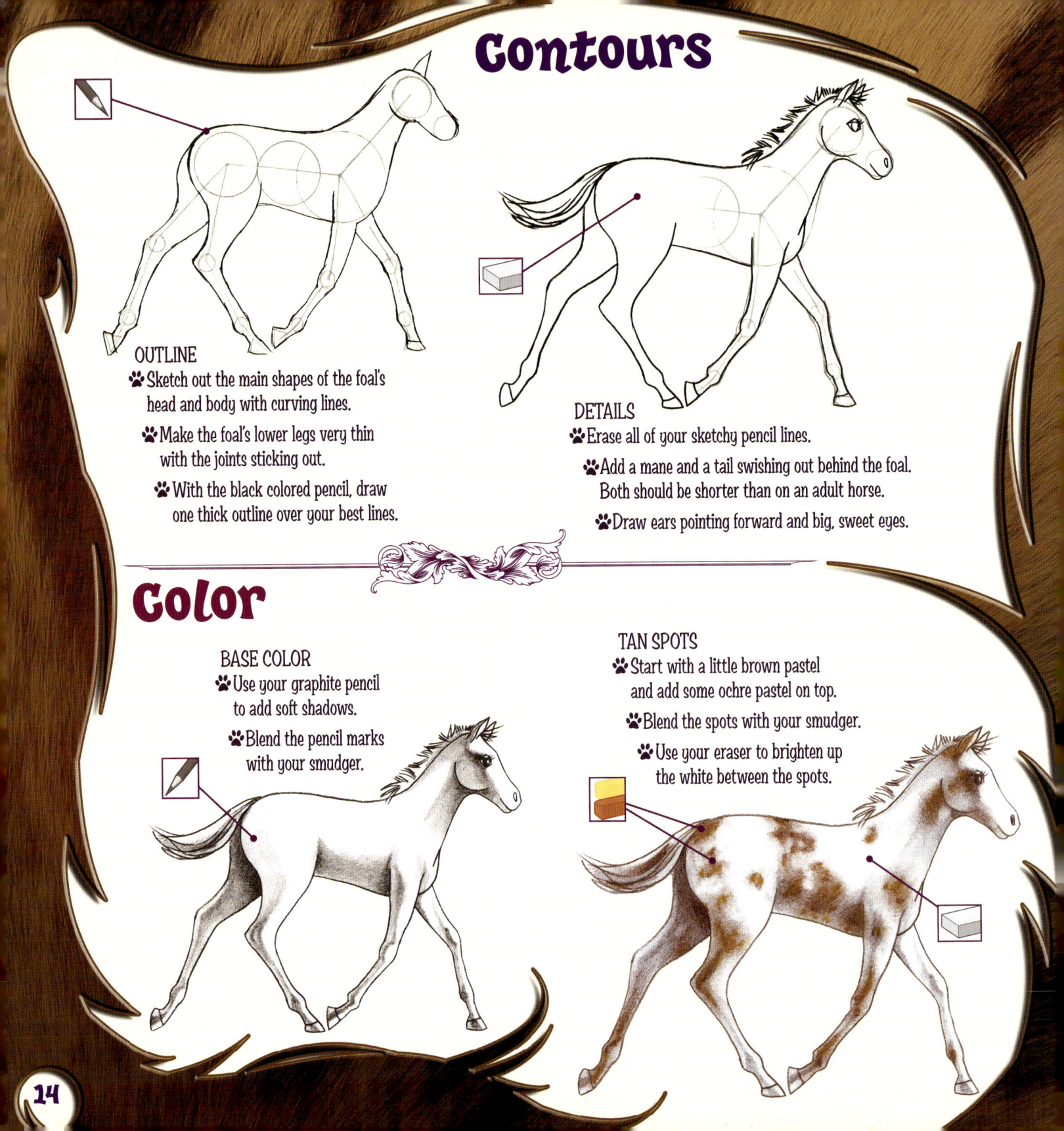

Contours

OUTLINE
- Sketch out the main shapes of the foal's head and body with curving lines.
- Make the foal's lower legs very thin with the joints sticking out.
- With the black colored pencil, draw one thick outline over your best lines.

DETAILS
- Erase all of your sketchy pencil lines.
- Add a mane and a tail swishing out behind the foal. Both should be shorter than on an adult horse.
- Draw ears pointing forward and big, sweet eyes.

Color

BASE COLOR
- Use your graphite pencil to add soft shadows.
- Blend the pencil marks with your smudger.

TAN SPOTS
- Start with a little brown pastel and add some ochre pastel on top.
- Blend the spots with your smudger.
- Use your eraser to brighten up the white between the spots.

Fun in the Sun

Put your foal on the beach at sunset. Start by lightly sketching the beach, water, island, and sky.

COLOR
- Use blue pastel for the sky and water.
- Create a sunset with light stripes of ochre and red pastel at the bottom of the sky.
- The sand and the island in the background are a mixture of ochre and brown pastel.

SMOOTH IT OUT
- Blend the color with your smudger.

ADD DETAIL
- Use brown pastel to make small dots on the back of the foal's legs, neck, and tail.
- Use your eraser to create clouds in the sky and waves in the water.

SHARPEN UP
- With the black colored pencil, go back over your black outlines.

Painted Pinto
You can try giving your foal larger spots, to make it a Pinto.

Foal on the Move
- Make three copies of your foal drawing.
- Cut out the body from one sheet.
- Cut out legs "A" and "C" from the second sheet, and "B" and "D" from the third sheet.
- Cut a slit near the top of each leg and in the body where the brads will go.
- Insert the brads, and let your foal take a walk!

A
B
C
D

15

Giddy Up!

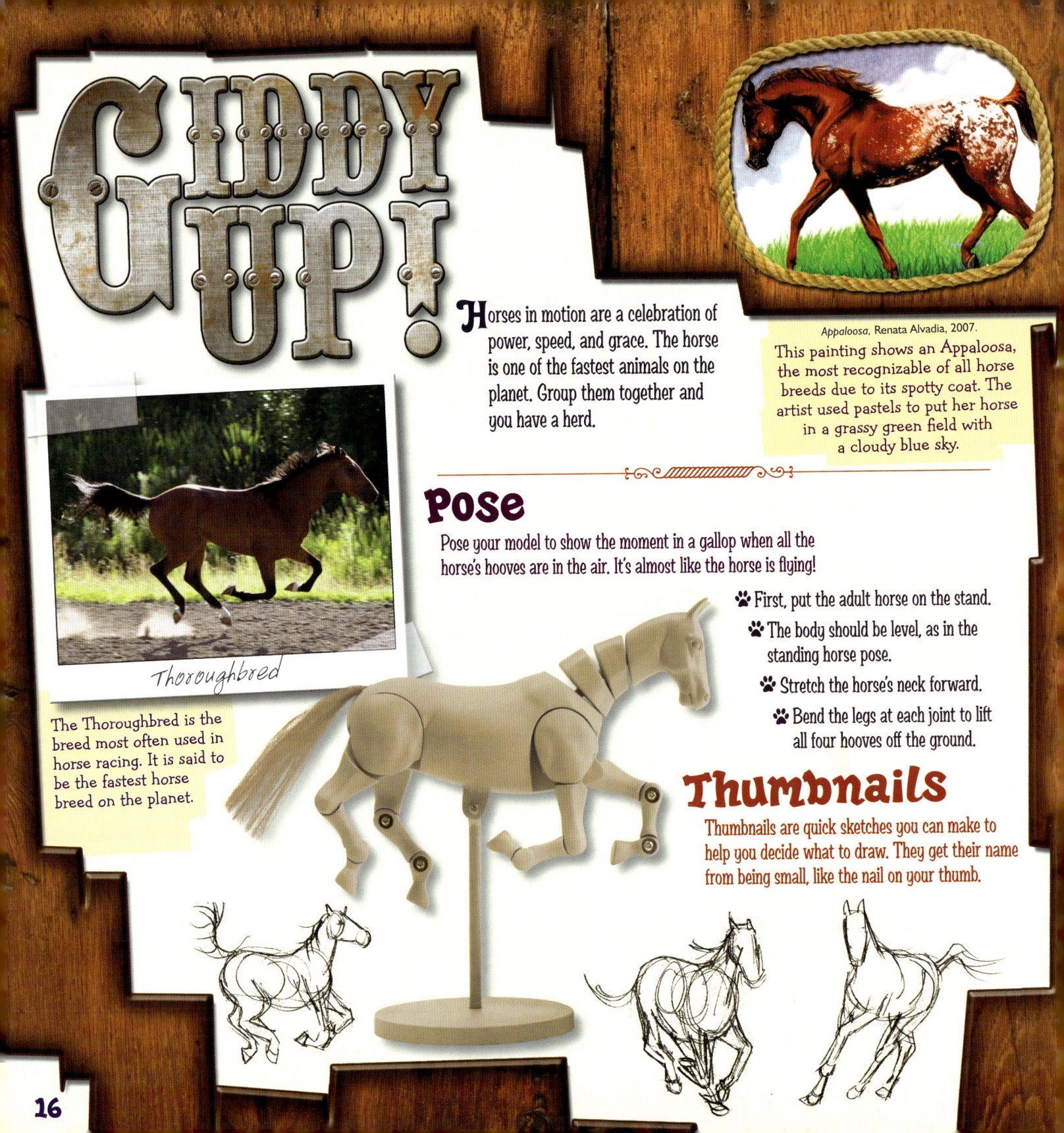

Horses in motion are a celebration of power, speed, and grace. The horse is one of the fastest animals on the planet. Group them together and you have a herd.

Appaloosa, Renata Alvadia, 2007.
This painting shows an Appaloosa, the most recognizable of all horse breeds due to its spotty coat. The artist used pastels to put her horse in a grassy green field with a cloudy blue sky.

Thoroughbred

The Thoroughbred is the breed most often used in horse racing. It is said to be the fastest horse breed on the planet.

Pose

Pose your model to show the moment in a gallop when all the horse's hooves are in the air. It's almost like the horse is flying!

- First, put the adult horse on the stand.
- The body should be level, as in the standing horse pose.
- Stretch the horse's neck forward.
- Bend the legs at each joint to lift all four hooves off the ground.

Thumbnails

Thumbnails are quick sketches you can make to help you decide what to draw. They get their name from being small, like the nail on your thumb.

Body & Head

Start this horse-in-motion just like you did for the Out of the Gait! project.

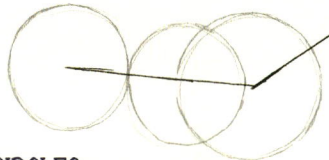

CIRCLES
🐾 Draw three circles for the body. Two side by side and a larger one in front.

EQUAL DISTANCE
🐾 Draw a line from the center of the back circle to the center of the front circle.

🐾 Draw another line of equal distance toward where the head will be.

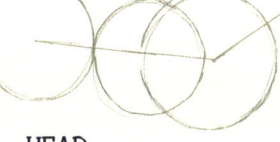

HEAD
🐾 Draw a circle at the top of the neckline for the head.

🐾 Draw a smaller circle for the tip of the muzzle.

REALITY CHECK

TWO-WAY STREET
Horses can see in two directions at once, but never directly in front or behind them.

REALITY CHECK

Legs & Contours

Study your model carefully to copy the position of the legs.

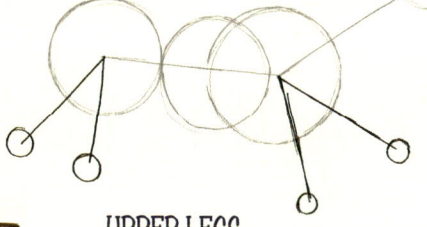

UPPER LEGS
🐾 Draw two lines from the center of the back circle.

🐾 Draw two lines from the center of the front circle.

🐾 Draw knee and hock circles at the ends of these lines.

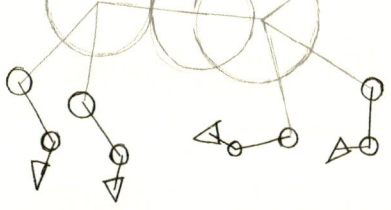

LOWER LEGS
🐾 Draw a line from each knee and each hock. These are the lower legs.

🐾 Draw circles for the fetlocks.

🐾 Draw four short lines for the pasterns and triangles for the hooves.

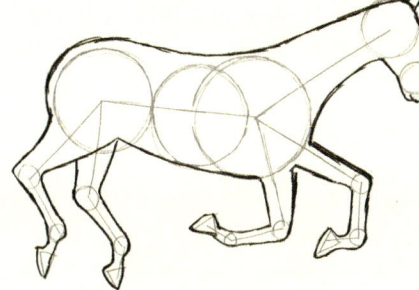

CONTOURS
🐾 Use curving lines to sketch the contours of the body, neck, and legs.

17

Details

- With a colored pencil, draw one thick outline over your best sketchy lines.
- Erase your sketchy pencil lines for a clean line drawing of your horse.
- Add details like the eye, mane, and tail.
- Make the mane and tail stream out behind the horse to show speed and motion.

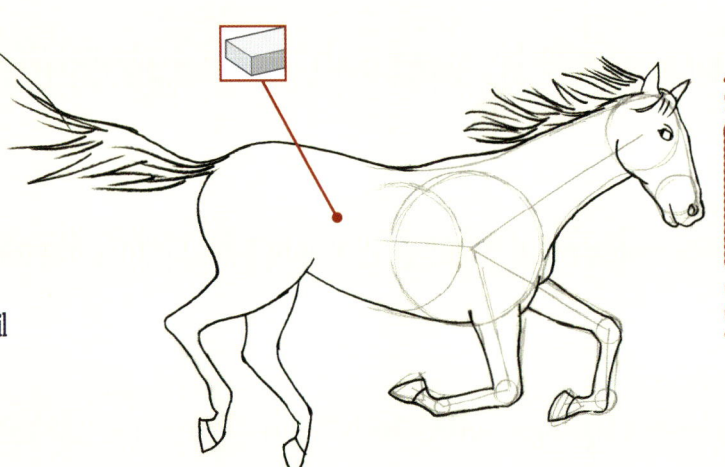

UNDER PRESSURE
Create flowing lines for your mane and tail. Press hard at the beginning of your line. Lighten up at the end to show the direction of motion.

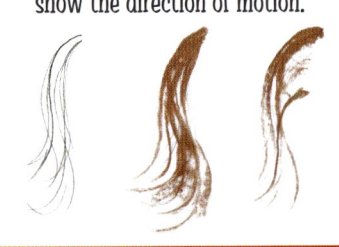

Color

A buckskin horse is sandy yellow with a dark brown mane and tail. These horses are known for toughness and strength. These qualities helped them survive in the Wild West.

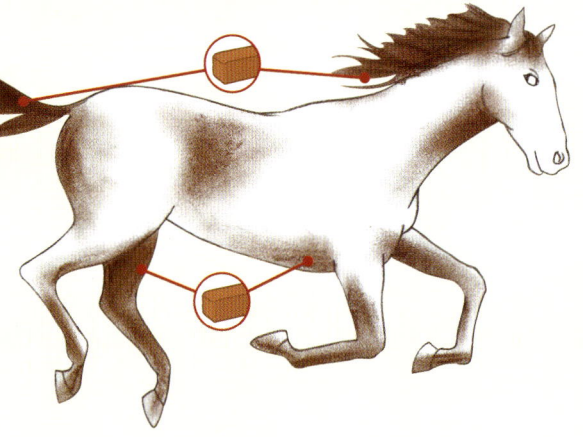

BASE COLOR
- Use brown pastel to color the mane and tail.
- Use more brown pastel for shading on the body, legs, and neck.

BUCKSKIN
- Add a layer of soft yellow pastel to give your horse a buckskin color.
- Smudge the mane and tail using your fingers or the smudger. This will help show motion.

SHOWING MOTION
Draw a simple picture of a person. Rub your fingers across your drawing in the direction it is moving away from.

Desert Bronco

Place your running bronco in the Wild West, with tumbleweeds and distant mountains.

DARKEN
Add more brown pastel and colored pencil to darken the legs, hips, and shoulders.

UNDER FOOT
Use ochre and brown pastel for the ground.

Use green pastel for the bushes.

Use brown pastel for the mountains.

Use blue pastel for the sky.

SMOOTH IT OUT
Use your smudger or a tissue to blend your colors.

SHADOWS
Use brown pastel to add a large shadow under the horse and shadows on the sides of the bushes.

SHARPEN UP
Add black colored pencil to the mane, tail, and outlines to sharpen up the drawing.

BRONCO BUSTIN'

Herd of Wild Horses
- Using your thumbnail sketches as a guide, add some other running horses to your drawing.
- Place them around, in front, and behind your first horse.
- Add lines for speed and sand for texture!

ARENA PATINA

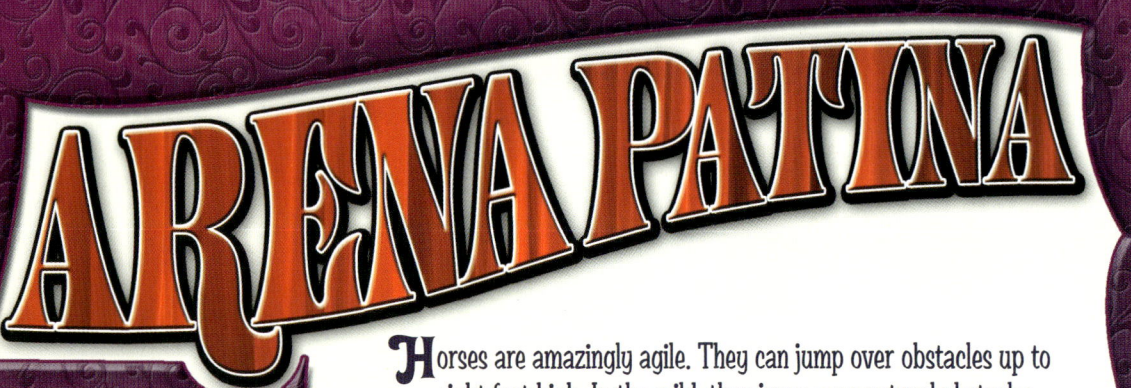

Horses are amazingly agile. They can jump over obstacles up to eight feet high. In the wild, they jump over natural obstacles. In competition, they jump over fences with riders on their backs. Horses also get to show off their amazing athletic talents in the show jumping arena. They complete complex obstacle courses of fences, moats, and other twists and turns.

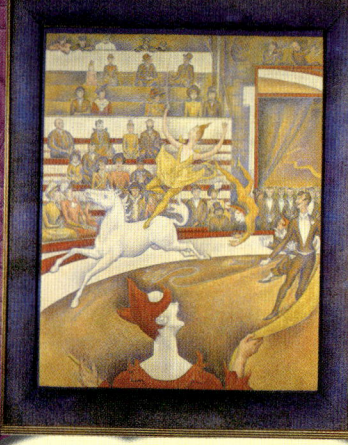

Le Cirque (The Circus), Georges Seurat, 1890. Seurat used thousands of tiny dots to fill in the colors in his paintings. This is called *pointillism*. It gives a vibrant feeling to this circus scene.

Lipizzaner

This horse was all black when it was born. Lipizzaners change color as they they grow up. They start out black and slowly turn "white" (actually gray) by the time they are six to ten years old. Even their mane and tail turn white. The horse in this picture is probably young because its mane is still dark gray.

Pose

This drawing is going to be showing a horse turned partly toward the front.

- Put the adult model on the stand and tilt up the front of the horse's body.
- Curl the front legs.
- Extend the back legs. Remember, all hooves should be in the air.
- Turn the stand so the horse faces you partway.

LINE 'EM UP

Imagine that your three circles are three tennis balls lined up in a row. If you tilt the row of tennis balls, your view of them changes.

You can see the entire ball in front but only part of the ones in back. When you turn your horse model, the same thing happens — the imaginary circles overlap.

Body & Head

If you look at your model from the front, the circles you use at the beginning of your drawing have turned in space. They now overlap.

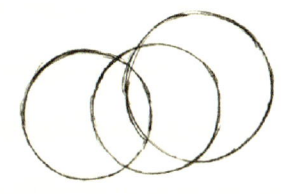

BODY
🐾 Draw overlapping circles, just like the turned row of tennis balls. The bigger circle should still be in front.

HEAD
🐾 Draw a line from the center of the back circle to the center of the front circle.

🐾 Draw a line of similar length for the neck.

🐾 Draw a circle at the top of the neck line for the head, and a circle for the muzzle.

CENTER LINE
🐾 Lengthen the line that goes through the body circles.

🐾 Divide the line into four sections.

🐾 Draw a dot at each section.

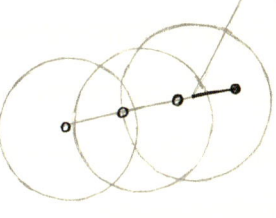

REALITY CHECK

Legs & Contours

For the jumping horse, the legs will be pointing in different directions.

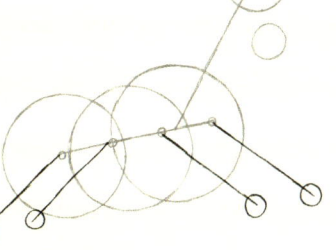

UPPER LEGS
🐾 Draw four lines for the upper legs, starting at the hips.

🐾 Point the front legs forward and the back legs backward.

🐾 Add small circles at the ends of these lines for the knees and hocks.

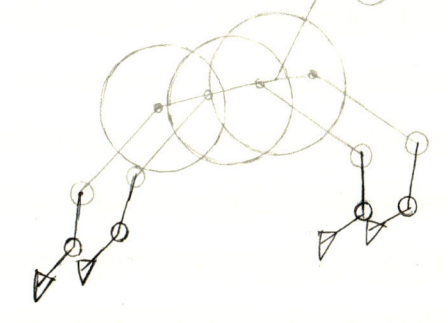

LOWER LEGS
🐾 Draw a line pointing down from each knee and each hock. These are the lower legs.

🐾 Sketch lines and circles for the pasterns and fetlocks. Draw triangles for hooves.

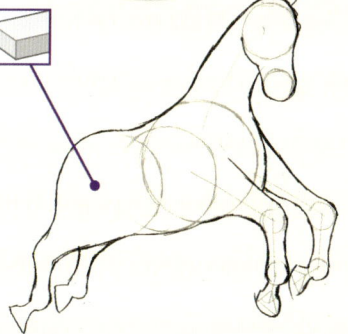

OUTLINE
🐾 Use curving lines to sketch the contours of the body, neck, and legs.

🐾 With a colored pencil, draw one thick outline over your best shapes.

🐾 Erase your sketchy pencil lines for a clean line drawing of your horse.

REALITY CHECK

Details

Our jumping horse is going to the circus!

- Add the horse's features: eyes, nose, mouth, and ears.
- Make the mane and tail flow behind the horse to show movement.
- Add as many fancy details as you can imagine—feather headress, harness, and leg wraps.
- Add a barrel. Learn how in the box to the right.

BARREL OF FUN

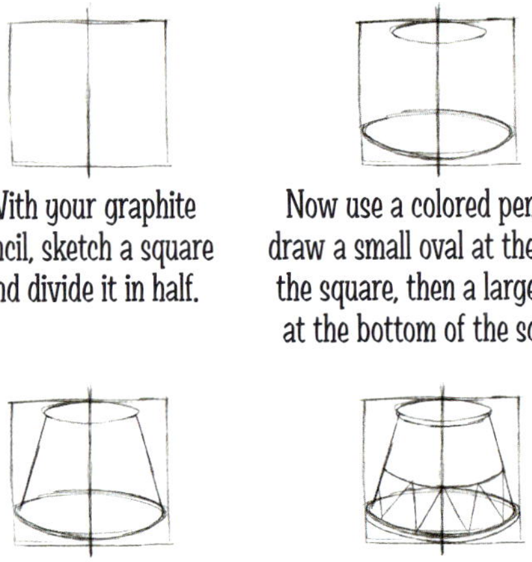

With your graphite pencil, sketch a square and divide it in half.

Now use a colored pencil to draw a small oval at the top of the square, then a larger oval at the bottom of the square.

Connect the two ovals with diagonal lines.

Add a row of triangles to the bottom of the barrel. Erase the square.

Color

Circus horses are often white. This shows off the bright colors of the harnesses and makes them visible from the grandstand.

SHADOWS
- Use your graphite pencil to blend soft shadows on the horse's body and legs, and on the barrel.

WHITE
- Leave the paper showing through to keep your horse bright white.

SHOW OFF
- Add color to the feathers, harness, and barrel.

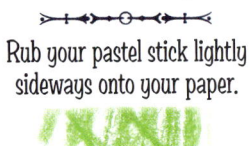

SOFT BLEND

For the feathers use this soft blend technique.

Rub your pastel stick lightly sideways onto your paper.

Rub your fingertip or a tissue over it to blend the marks together.

Circus Fun

Sketch the basic lines for the floor, audience, and tent of this circus scene.

UNDER FOOT
Yellow pastel creates a sandy floor.

RING
Blue pastel and black colored pencil darken the edge of the circus ring.

SMOOTH IT OUT
Blend a light layer of purple and brown pastel to show the grandstand.

ERASER
Use your eraser to make light dots to show the audience.

STRIPES
Add red stripes behind the audience. This is the circus tent.

FRONT TO BACK
Have you noticed how things get blurry when they are farther away? Try to recreate this effect in your drawing.

ENCORE!

Ring of Fire
Circus animals perform daring acts. Draw another jumping horse sailing through a ring of fire.

Horse Puppet
Glue your drawing onto some thin cardboard. Cut it out and glue your horse on a popsicle stick.

23

FANTASTICAL

The unicorn lives in stories and imaginations. Though unicorns seem impossibly magical, they are not much different from real horses. What is the difference between a horse and a unicorn? The horn! You can add a horn to any horse drawing to create a unicorn.

The Unicorn in Captivity, South Netherlandish, circa 1500.

This tapestry of silk and wool shows a scene of a unicorn inside of a fence, lying next to a pomegranate tree. It tells the story of a magical creature happily in love. The unicorn could easily jump the low fence, but it stays to enjoy the fruit from the tree.

Pose

Let's draw a horse in a rearing position. Rearing is what horses do when they get excited.

POSE
🐾 Put the horse model on the stand and tilt the front of the body up. Keep the back hooves on the ground.

Arabian

The Arabian is known for its courage and speed. Walter Farley's *Black Stallion* novels and films are about an Arabian horse.

Thumbnails

Try your hand at some rearing poses. Turn the model so you can see it from different angles.

24

Main Body

This pose looks like the standing pose, but it's tilted up. In this pose the circles are stacked on top of each other.

BODY
- Draw the circles for the body.

EQUAL DISTANCE
- Draw a line from the center of the back circle to the center of the front circle.

- Draw a line of equal distance for the neck-line. It is almost straight up.
- Draw a circle for the head on the top of this line.
- Add a circle for the muzzle.

LEG ROOM
- Draw two lines pointing downward from the back circle. Add small circles for the hocks.
- Draw two lines pointing forward from the front circle. Add small circles for the knees.

REALITY CHECK

Legs & Contours

Finish your horse's legs by carefully studying your model first.

LEGS
- Draw lines for the lower legs.
- Draw circles for the fetlocks.
- Draw lines for the pasterns and triangles for the hooves.

OUTLINE
- Sketch in the contours of the body, neck, and legs using curving lines.
- With a colored pencil, draw one thick outline over your best sketchy lines.
- Erase all the sketchy pencil lines so you have a clean line drawing of your horse.

REALITY CHECK

MYSTICAL

Unicorns are supposed to be especially wild and hard to tame, so a rearing pose is a perfect way to show the unicorn's personality.

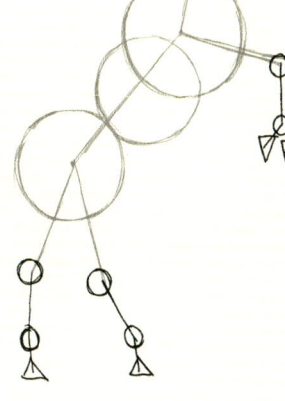

Details

Add details like the eyes, tail, mane, and a horn! Make the tail and mane flow downward and behind the horse to show motion.

UNICORN HORN
Drawing a horn is easy.

Draw a straight line pointing out of the top of your horse's head.

Draw two diagonal lines to make a triangle.

Add stripes across the cone and thicken each section.

UNICORN EYES
You can draw the eyes with a few simple lines.

Looking forward | Looking down | Looking up | From the side | Sleepy eyes

Color

The graphite and rose colored pencils will give your unicorn a mystical look.

SHADING
❧ Use your graphite pencil to blend soft shadows on the horse's legs, body, and horn.

MAKE IT PINK
❧ Cover the graphite with a smooth, light layer of rose colored pencil.

LIGHT IT UP
Turn the lights off in your room. Shine a flashlight on your model to show strong shadows and bright highlights.

DETAILS
❧ Leave the highlights white.
❧ Add extra rose to the mane, horn, and tail.

Starry Night

A nicorn should be in a magical landscape. Sketch a landscape of mountains, lake, and moon.

LOOSE COLOR
Use your purple pastel to fill in the sky and the lake. Leave white areas for the stars, the moon, and the glowing area around the horn.

FOREGROUND TEXTURE
Place your paper on a rough surface like an old table or piece of wood.

Hold your brown pastel on its side. When you rub, you will see the texture of the wood come through.

Add more brown for the horse's shadow.

SMOOTH IT OUT
Use your smudger to blend the pastel marks.

CLEAN IT UP
Use your eraser to clean up the white areas, like the reflection of the moon on the water.

ART TIP!
Use a second piece of paper to keep smudges off of your drawing. Place the clean piece of paper on top of your drawing, under your hand. This helps prevent smearing.

GLOW ON!

Rainbow Glow
Create a new kind of magic horse. How about a horse with a rainbow mane? A white foal right next to it can reflect the rainbow colors.

Glow Horse
Add glitter glue to your starry night unicorn.

27

CARTOON corral

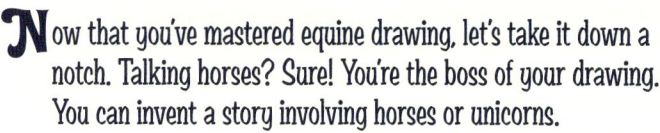

Now that you've mastered equine drawing, let's take it down a notch. Talking horses? Sure! You're the boss of your drawing. You can invent a story involving horses or unicorns.

Horses under a Willow Tree (Ryuka No Uma), Shunsen Katsukawa, circa 1830.
This Japanese woodcut shows two horses in a loose, playful style. To create this image, the artist didn't spend too much time worrying about the horses' measurements. The artist probably drew horses until he could draw them from memory!

Pose and Thumbnails

Your poses don't have to be real-life horse poses. Have some fun with the models.

POSE
- Pose your horse and foal as if they were at a tea party.
- Practice drawing thumbnails of your poses.

ART TIP!
Cartoon colors are bright and simple, so don't worry about shading. Just pick a few areas of your drawing and fill them in with solid color. When you keep the colors simple, the lines stand out.

Body & Details

For cartoon horses, use the same basic methods you've learned from all the other projects.

CIRCLES AND LINES
- Draw some quick circles and lines that match the pose of your models.

DETAILS
- Sketch curving lines to show the contours of the horse heads and bodies.
- Draw details like the teapot and teacups to finish the scene.

EXPRESSIVE EYES
Here's a few different types of eyes you can draw!

COLOR IT!
- Use ochre pastel and rose colored pencil to fill in the horse bodies.
- Use purple and ochre pastel for details like manes, tails, and hooves.
- Use blue pastel for teapot and teacups.
- Use red pastel to create the squares of the picnic blanket.
- Add green pastel for the background.
- Sharpen up the outlines with black colored pencil.

Letting Go of the Reins

Little Blue Horse, Franz Marc, 1912

This vivid painting uses color in an unrealistic way. Horses aren't blue, and the landscape is not really hot pink, neon orange, and cherry red. But when the artist put all of these bright colors together, he created something very real—a picture that expresses an emotion.

Now that you've mastered realistic drawing techniques, it's time to let go of the reins and have some creative fun. Gather all of your tools together and get ready to make a lively, colorful horse drawing.

Bucking Foal

This bucking foal has a white marking on its back right leg. It is called a sock because it only goes halfway up the leg. If it went to the joint, it would be called a stocking.

Pose and Thumbnails

Let's use an energetic bucking foal for this drawing. A frolicking foal is a perfect model for breaking things up and having fun.

POSE
- Put the foal model on the stand and tilt the body forward.
- Keep the front legs pointing forward on the ground, but point the back legs up in the air.

SKETCH
- Using your black colored pencil, practice drawing circles and lines.
- Draw thumbnail sketches of your pose. Let the shapes be disconnected and free.

ART TIP!
Think about the shapes you used to draw the other horses. Use circles and lines, but don't worry about getting the shapes and sizes right.

30

Young Buck

Sketch out your horse, or jump right in with your pastels.

COLOR
Use ochre pastel for the body and head. Blend it smooth with your smudger or your finger.

LAYER
Layer brown and red pastel over the ochre on the neck and rear. Let the ochre show through in spots. Experiment with blending or keeping the lines bold.

DETAILS
Make fast curving strokes with the black colored pencil for the body. Draw the eye.

KEEP GOING
Use rose colored pencil to add color to the chest and rear. Use red pastel to create bold lines for the mane, muzzle, and cheek.

BACKGROUND
Use blue and green pastel for the sky and field.

MORE POP!

Curly Swirls
Use all your pastels to create this swirly abstract horse.

Collage Me
Cut out shapes from construction paper and magazines. Glue them on a scenic background. Add string, buttons, etc. for a 3-D effect.

31

ROUND-UP

You've drawn simple versions of horses in every type of pose. Now you can use your model to see your horse from other angles. Take your horses on adventures. Imagine new kinds of backgrounds, magical and real. Now that you know how to start a horse with circles and lines, you can draw any pose!

HORSE BALLET
Your cartoon horses can dance in the ballet. Give them frilly costumes!

FLY AWAY
Try drawing a different magical horse, like a Pegasus. Make its wings any color you want.

RODEO KING
Are you in a rough-and-tumble mood? Send your bucking horse to the rodeo.

FLOWER GIRL
Baby horses love flowers! Give your foal a field of daisies.

BLAZE ON!

Don't stop here. This isn't the end, it's just the beginning!